The Pleasure Of Your Company

at the playing of

Piano Duets

is requested
by

Melvin Stecher,
Norman Horowitz
& Claire Gordon

ISBN 978-0-634-01604-2

G. SCHIRMER, Inc.

DISTRIBUTED BY

HAL•LEONARD®
CORPORATION

7777 W. BLUEMOUND RD. P.O. BOX 13819 MILWAUKEE, WI 53213

RIPPLING RIVER

Secondo

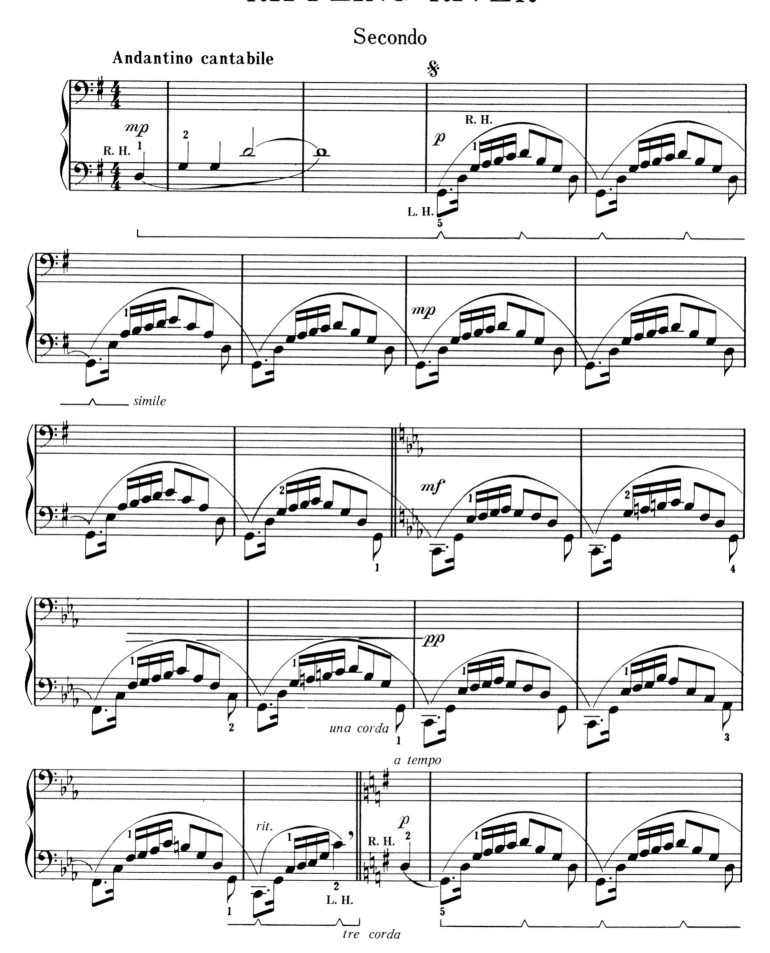

RIPPLING RIVER

Primo

Andantino cantabile

Secondo

Primo

SUPERSTARS AND STRIPES

Secondo

Tempo di marcia con spirito

SUPERSTARS AND STRIPES

Primo

Tempo di marcia con spirito

8

Secondo

Primo

DMITRI'S DREAM

Secondo

Andante con passióne

DMITRI'S DREAM

Primo

Andante con passióne

Secondo

Primo

Secondo

Primo

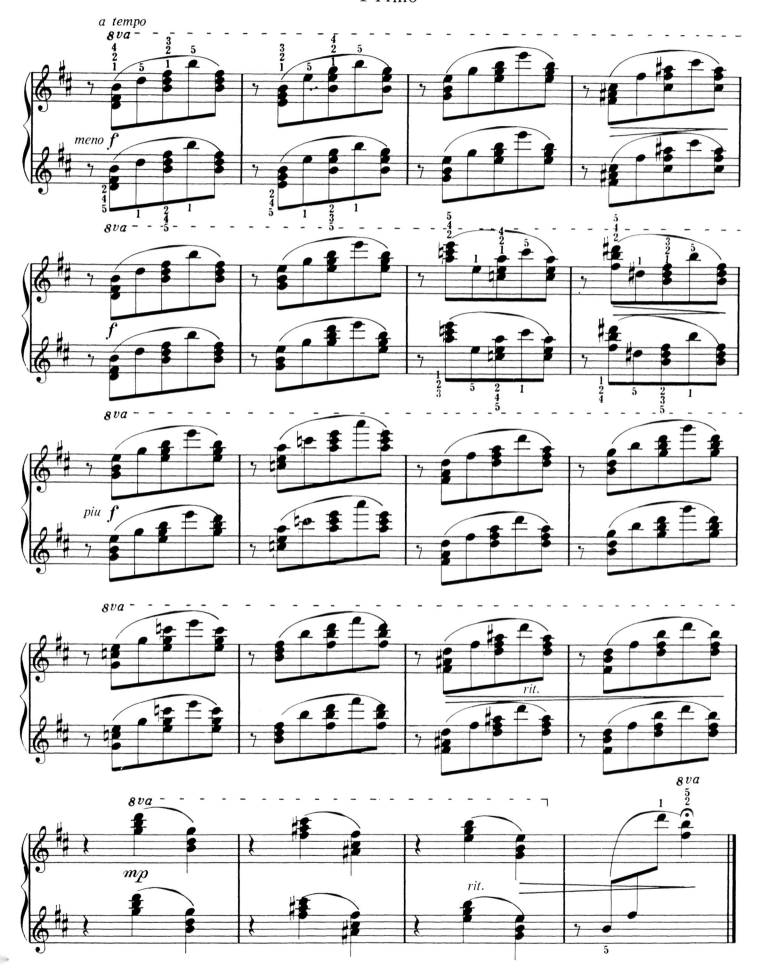